THE KIDS' BOOK OF MAZES 1

Dr Gareth Moore B.Sc (Hons) M.Phil Ph.D
is an Ace Puzzler, and author of lots of puzzle books.
He created an online brain-training site called
BrainedUp.com, and runs an online puzzle site
called PuzzleMix.com. Gareth has a PhD from
the University of Cambridge, where he taught
machines to understand spoken English.

Buster Books

Revised paperback edition first published in 2017

First published in Great Britain in 2014 by Buster Books,
an imprint of Michael O'Mara Books Limited,
9 Lion Yard, Tremadoc Road, London SW4 7NQ

www.busterbooks.co.uk   Buster Children's Books   @BusterBooks

Illustrations and layouts © Buster Books 2014, 2017
Bridge and circular mazes and solutions © Gareth Moore 2014, 2017
All other mazes generated by www.mazegenerator.net

Illustrations by John Bigwood and Sarah Horne

A CIP catalogue record for this book is available from the British Library.

ISBN: 978-1-78055-500-3

1 3 5 7 9 10 8 6 4 2

Papers used by Buster Books are natural, recyclable products
made from wood grown in sustainable forests. The manufacturing processes
conform to the environmental regulations of the country of origin.

Puzzles designed and typeset by Dr Gareth Moore
www.drgarethmoore.com

Layout designed by Barbara Ward

Printed and bound in April 2017 by CPI Group (UK) Ltd,
108 Beddington Lane, Croydon, CR0 4YY, United Kingdom

Contents

Amazing Mazes!

Mazes are puzzles that absolutely anyone can solve. They come in loads of different shapes and sizes, and all you need to complete them is a pen or pencil.

Find your way

A maze may look like a simple puzzle, but it can be very tough to solve. The mazes in this book are made up of branching passages through which the solver – that's you! – must find a route, from the 'In' to the 'Out'.

Whether the pathways in a maze are rectangular, triangular, hexagonal or circular, the walls are fixed, so you cannot jump over them. If you come to a dead end, you can only turn around or go back to the beginning and try again.

As some mazes may take you more than one try to solve, you might want to use a pencil so you can rub out your lines if you need to start again. But you can use a pen if you are feeling more confident.

Are you a beginner or the best?

The mazes in this book get tougher as the book progresses. There are four separate difficulty levels, which are shown at the top of each page. There's also a 'Time' line where you can fill in exactly how long it has taken you to solve each maze.

How to solve a bridge maze

A bridge maze is a type of maze that includes bridges. This allows the solution path to cross over and under itself. Have a look at this example, which shows how bridges work. They can make a maze a lot trickier to solve, and it's much easier to miss a potential route.

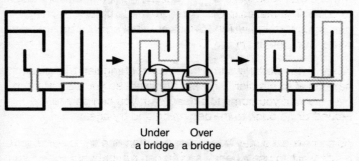

Under   Over
a bridge   a bridge

Introducing the Puzzle Master, Dr Gareth Moore

Dr Gareth Moore B.Sc (Hons) M.Phil Ph.D, who created the bridge and circular mazes in this book, is an Ace Puzzler, and author of lots of puzzle and brain-training books.

He created an online brain-training site called BrainedUp.com, and runs an online puzzle site called PuzzleMix.com. Gareth has a PhD from the University of Cambridge, where he taught machines to understand spoken English.

Level One:
Beginners

Time ....

Maze 1

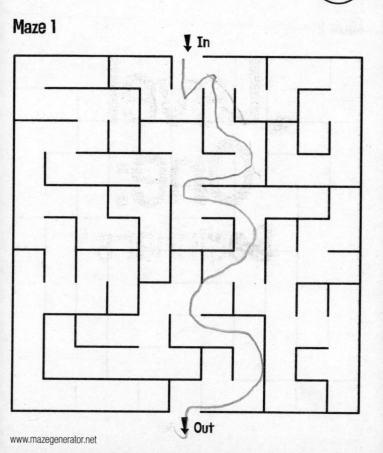

Maze 2

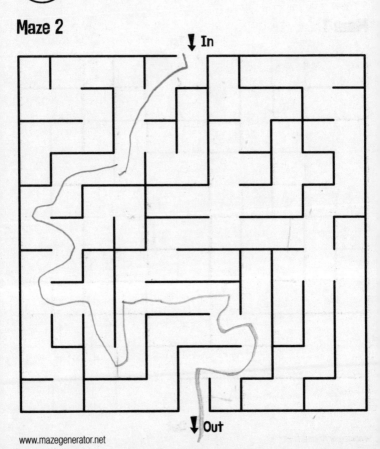

Maze 3

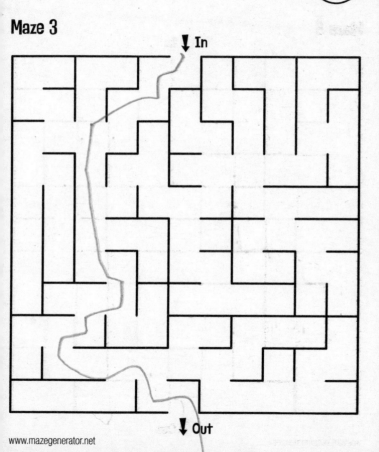

Maze 4

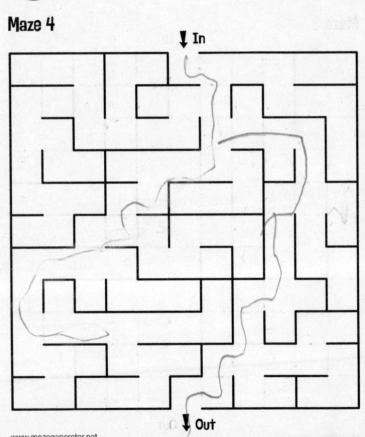

↓ In

↓ Out

Maze 5

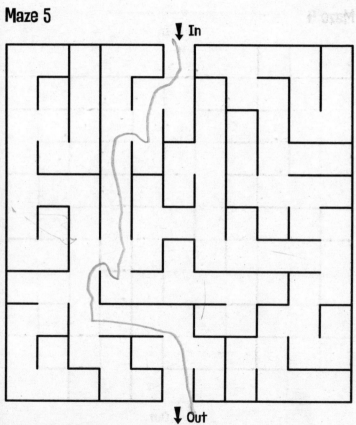

Maze 6

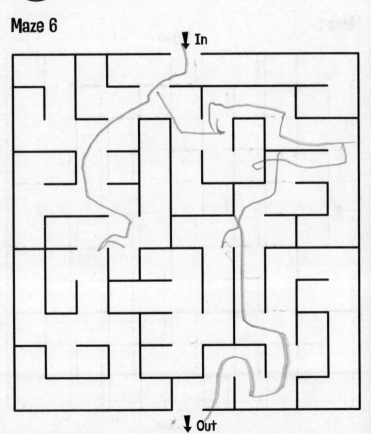

Maze 7

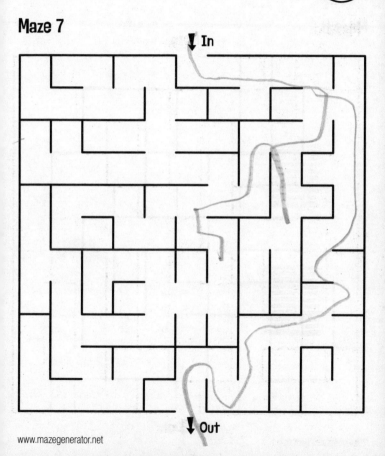

Maze 8

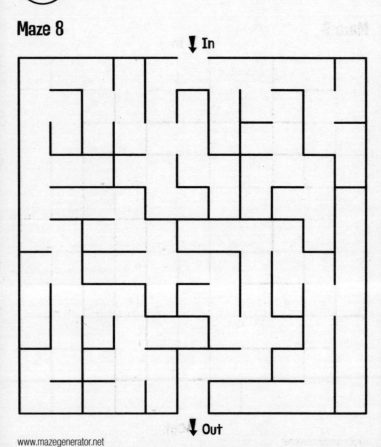

Maze 9

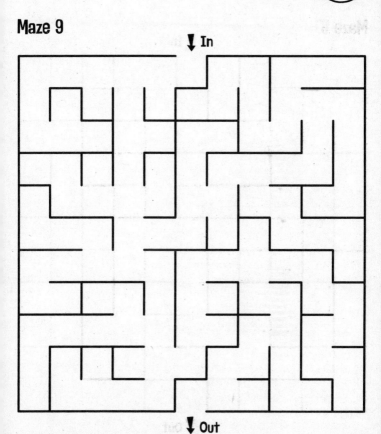

Maze 10

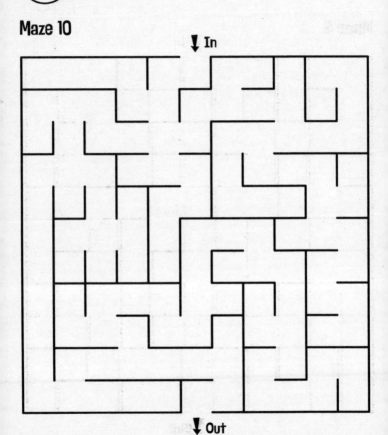

↓ In

↓ Out

Maze 11

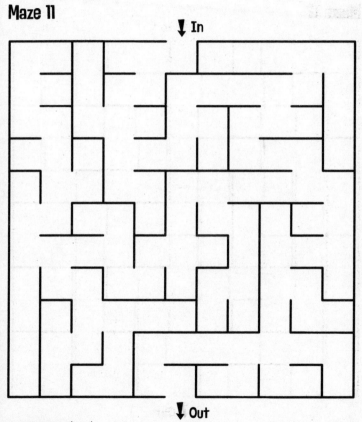

 Time ....

Maze 12

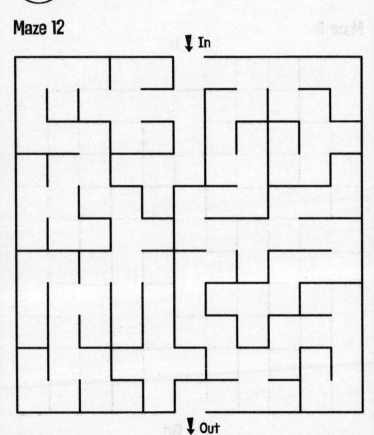

↓ In

↓ Out

Maze 13

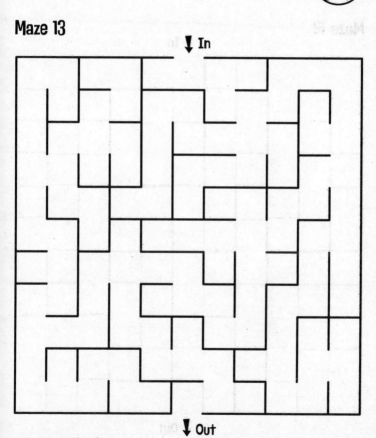

Maze 14

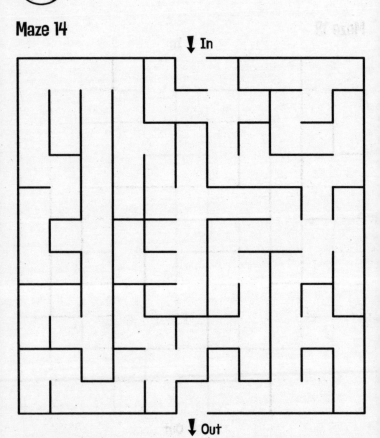

Maze 15

↓ **In**

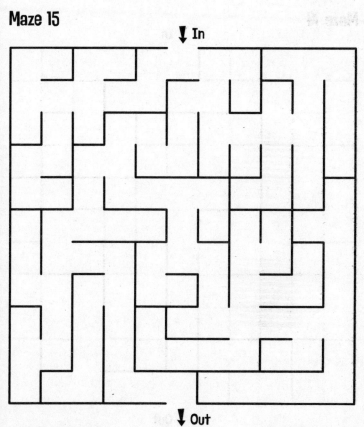

↓ **Out**

Maze 16

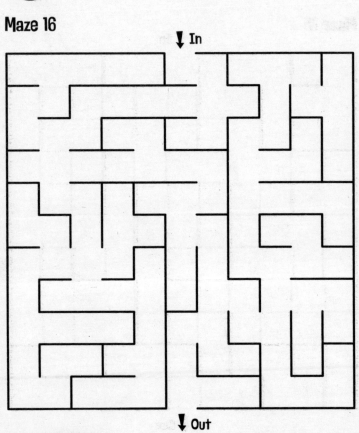

↓ In

↓ Out

Maze 17

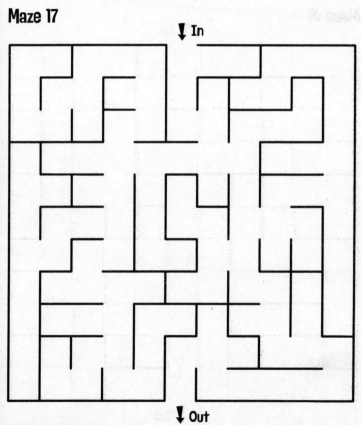

↓ In

↓ Out

Maze 18

↓ In

↓ Out

Maze 19

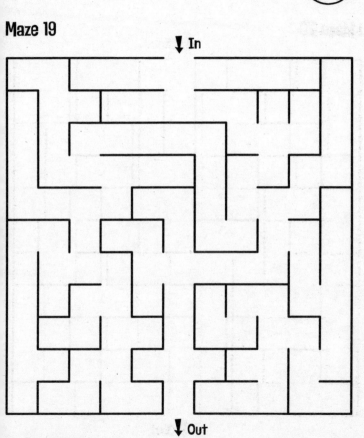

↓ In

↓ Out

Maze 20

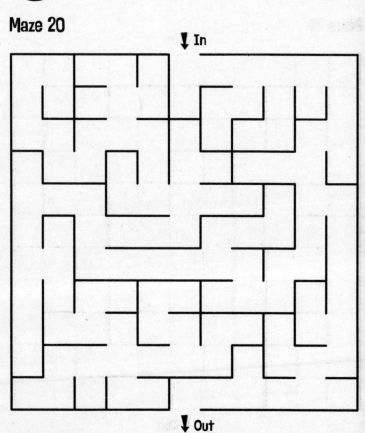

↓ In

↓ Out

Maze 21

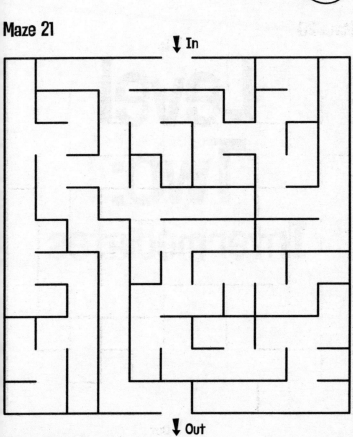

Level Two:
Intermediates

Maze 22

Maze 23

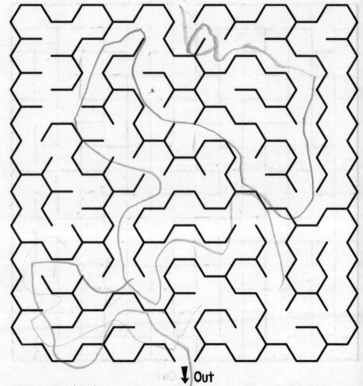

↓ In

↓ Out

Maze 24

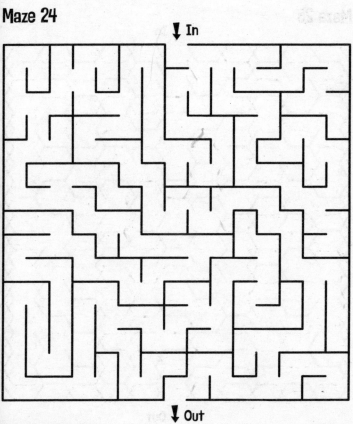

Maze 25

In

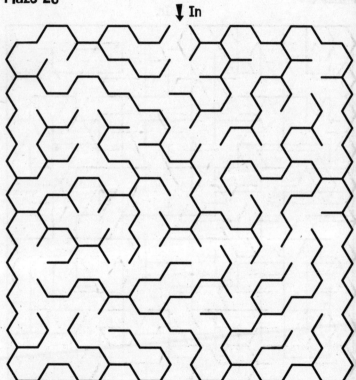

Out

Maze 26

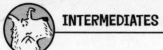

Maze 27

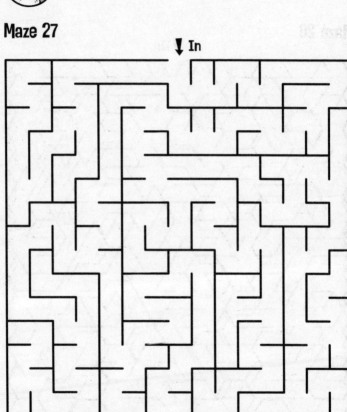

Maze 28

↓ In

↓ Out

Maze 29

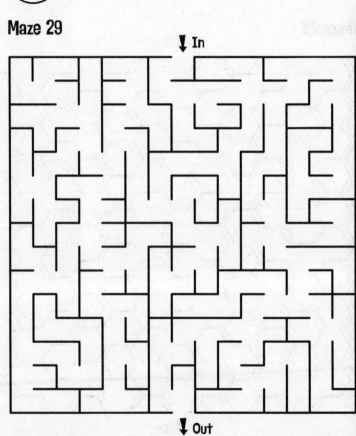

Maze 30

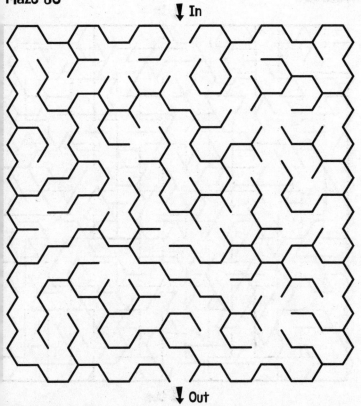

↓ In

↓ Out

Maze 31

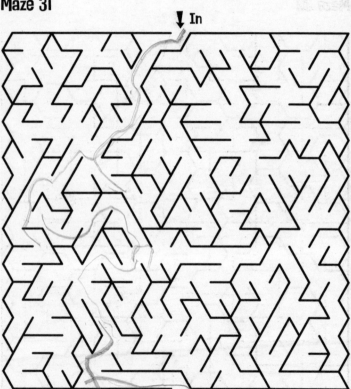

↓ In

↓ Out

Maze 32

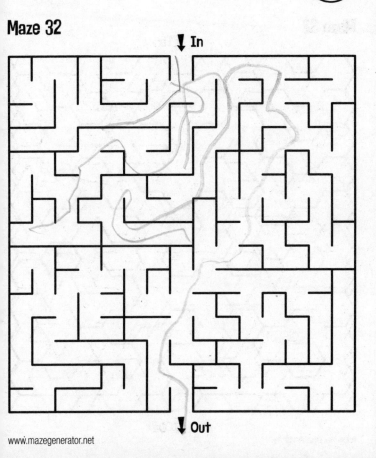

Maze 33

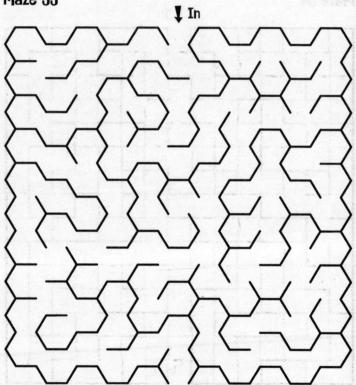

Maze 34

↓ In

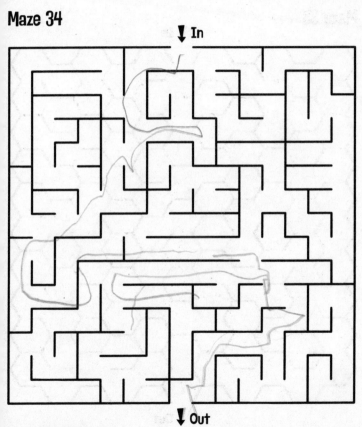

↓ Out

Maze 35

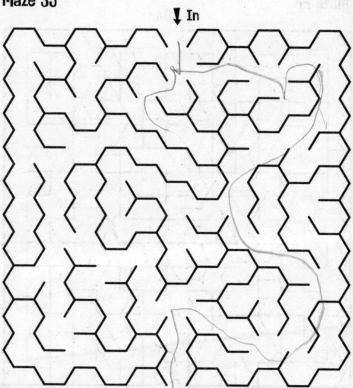

In

Out

Maze 36

↓ In

↓ Out

Maze 37

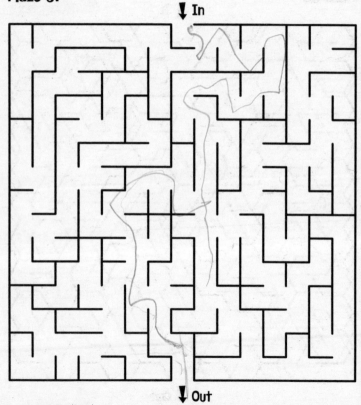

Maze 38

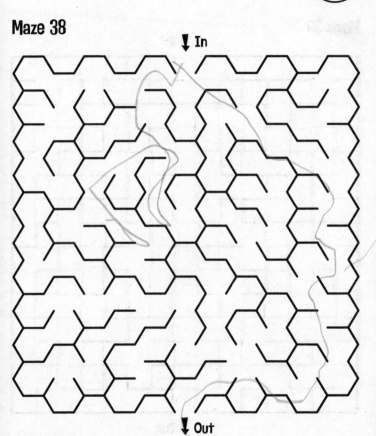

Maze 39

↓ In

↓ Out

Maze 40

In

Out

Maze 41

↓ In

↓ Out

Maze 42

↓ In

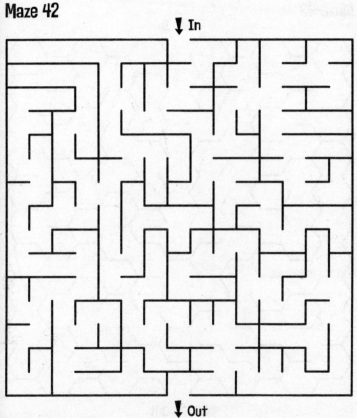

↓ Out

Maze 43

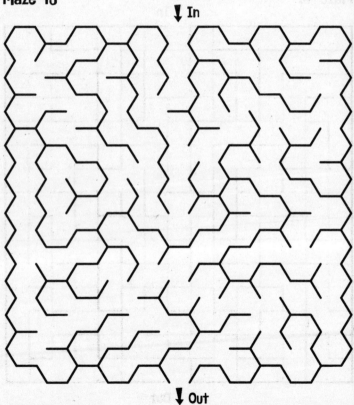

↓ In

↓ Out

Maze 44

↓ **In**

↓ **Out**

Maze 45

 In

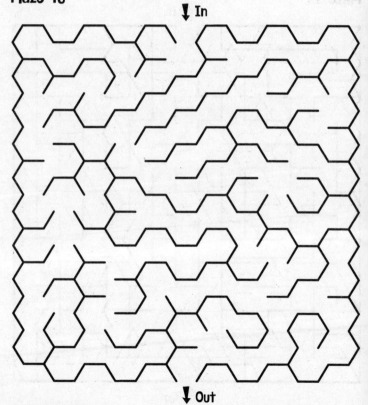

Out

Maze 46

↓ In

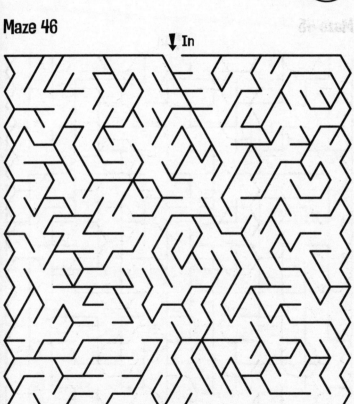

↓ Out

INTERMEDIATES Time...

Maze 47

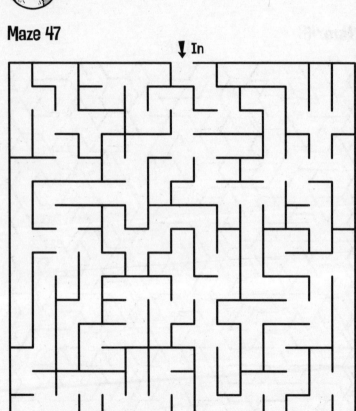

Maze 48

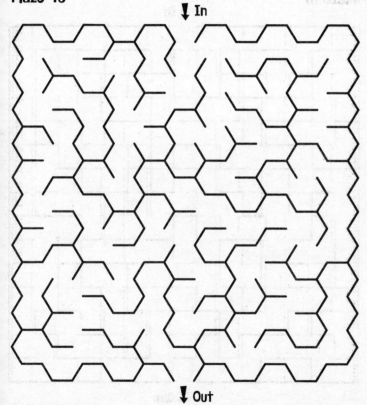

Time ....

Maze 49

↓ In

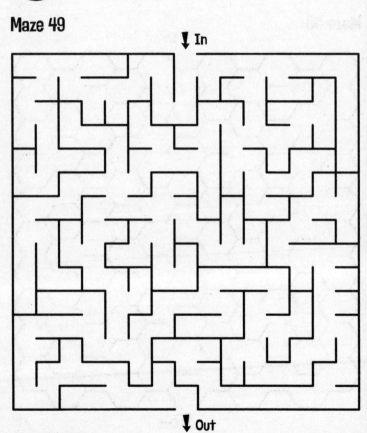

↓ Out

Maze 50

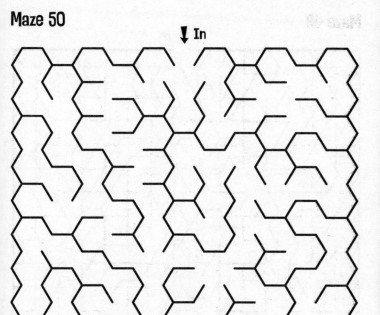

Maze 51

↓ In

↓ Out

Maze 52

↓ **In**

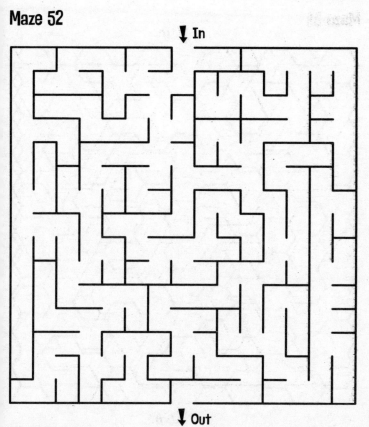

↓ **Out**

Maze 53

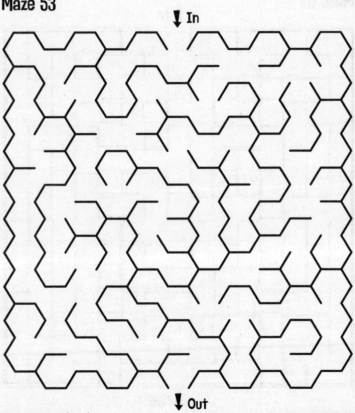

In

Out

Maze 54

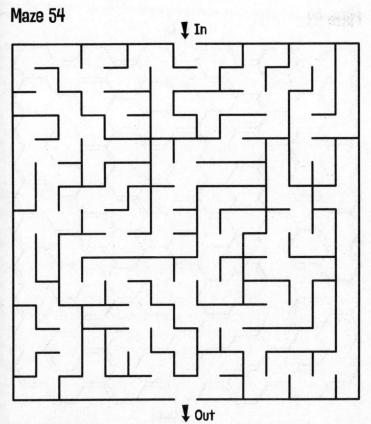

Maze 55

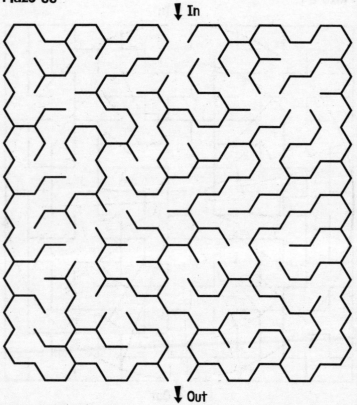

Maze 56

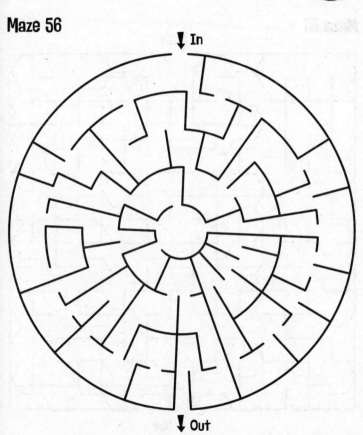

Maze 57

▼ In

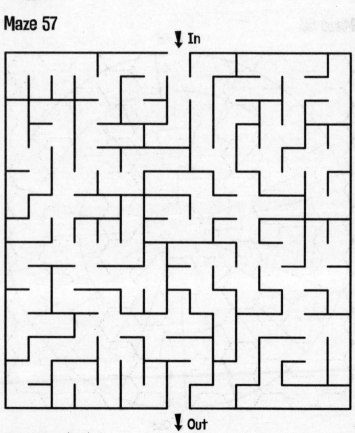

▼ Out

Maze 58

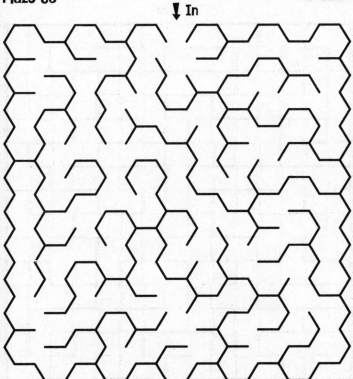

Maze 59

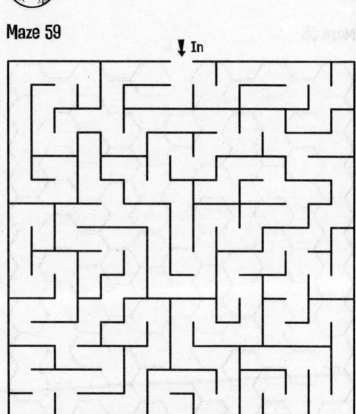

Maze 60

↓ **In**

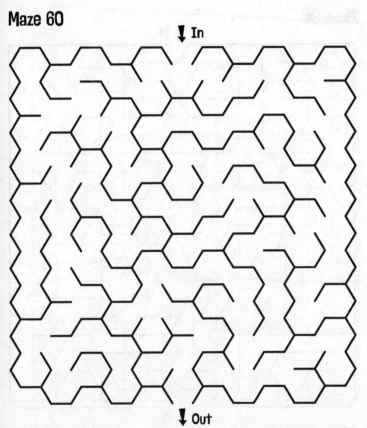

↓ **Out**

Maze 61

↓ **In**

↓ **Out**

Maze 62

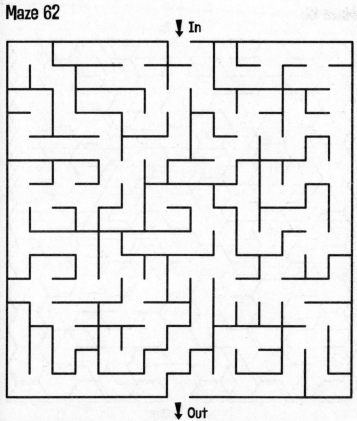

Maze 63

↓ In

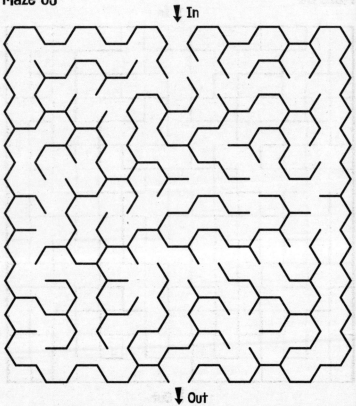

↓ Out

Maze 64

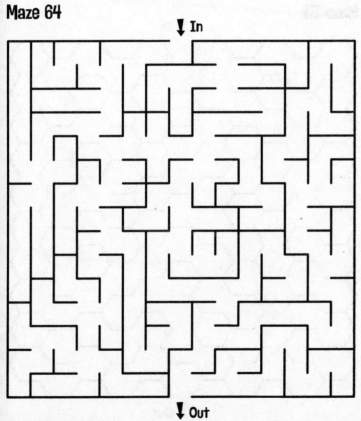

Maze 65

↓ In

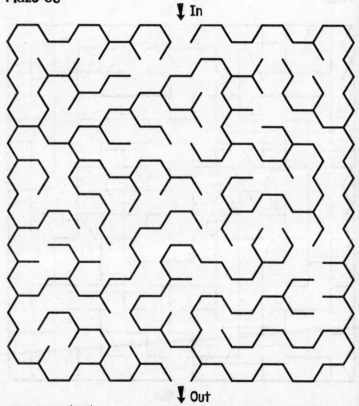

↓ Out

Maze 66

↓ **In**

↓ **Out**

Maze 67

Maze 68

In

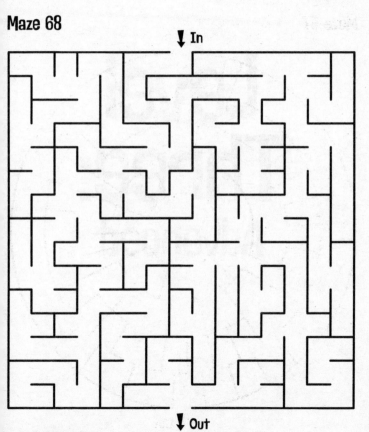

Out

Level
Three:
Advanced

Maze 69

▼ In

▼ Out

Time ....

Maze 70

↓ In

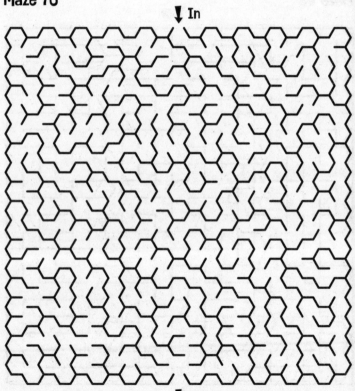

↓ Out

Maze 71

In

Out

Maze 72

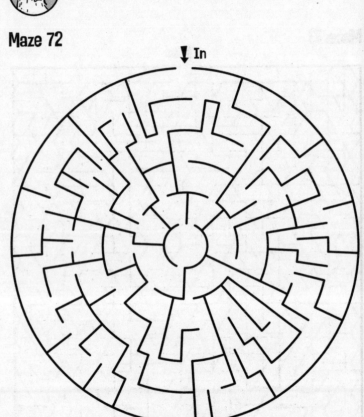

Maze 73

Maze 74

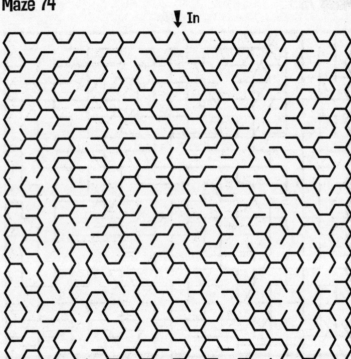

↓ In

↓ Out

Maze 75

▼ In

▼ Out

Time ....

Maze 76

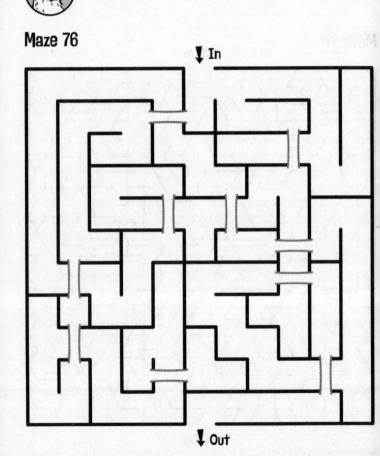

Maze 77

↓ In

↓ Out

Maze 78

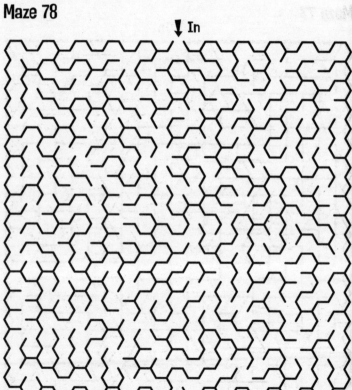

In

Out

Maze 79

↓ In

↓ Out

Maze 80

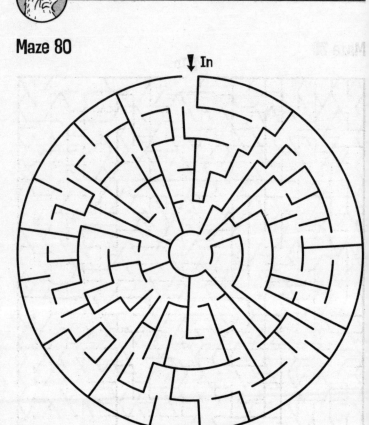

Maze 81

Maze 82

Time ....

Maze 83

↓ In

↓ Out

Maze 84

 In

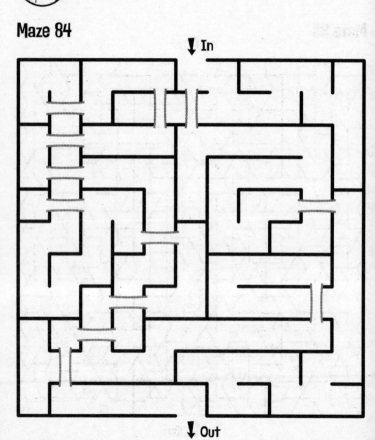

↓ Out

Maze 85

↓ In

↓ Out

 **ADVANCED** Time ....

Maze 86

In

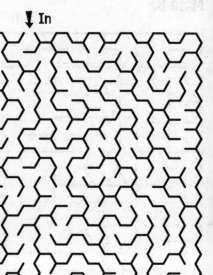

Out

Maze 87

▼ In

▼ Out

Maze 88

Maze 89

↓ In

↓ Out

Maze 90

In

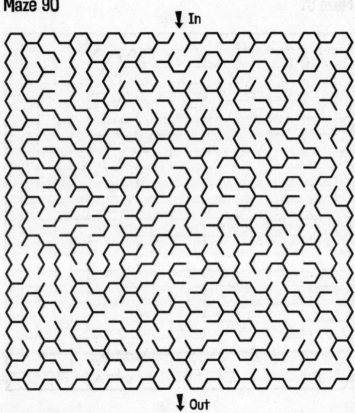

Out

Maze 91

▼ In

▼ Out

Maze 92

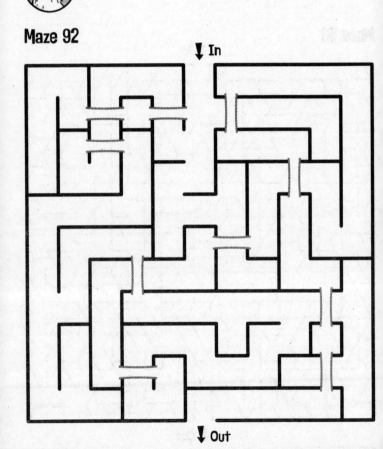

Maze 93

↓ **In**

↓ **Out**

Maze 94

↓ In

↓ Out

Maze 95

In

Out

Maze 96

Maze 97

↓ In

↓ Out

Maze 98

Maze 99

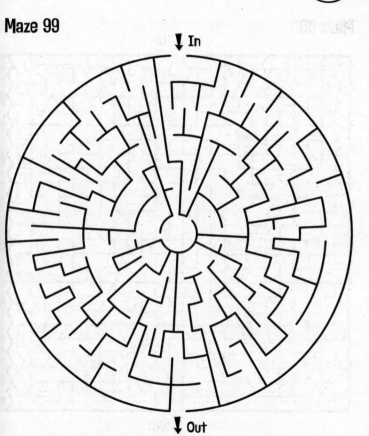

Maze 100

Maze 101

↓ In

↓ Out

 **ADVANCED** Time ....

Maze 102

▼ In

▼ Out

Maze 103

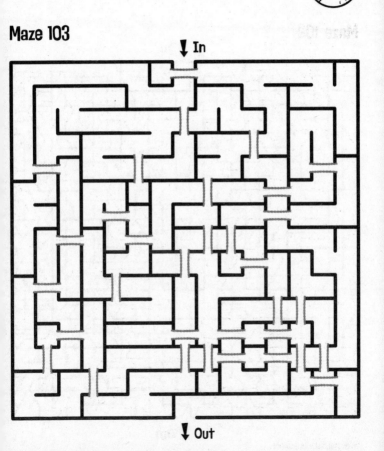

Maze 104

↓ In

↓ Out

Maze 105

▼ In

▼ Out

Maze 106

↓ In

↓ Out

Maze 107

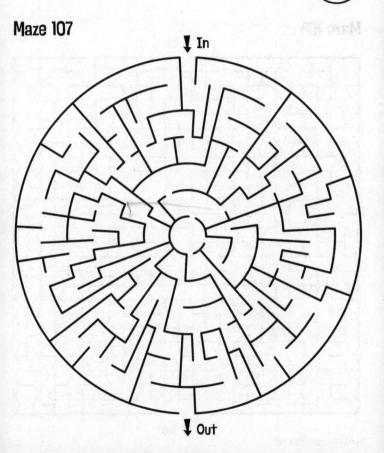

↓ In

↓ Out

Maze 108

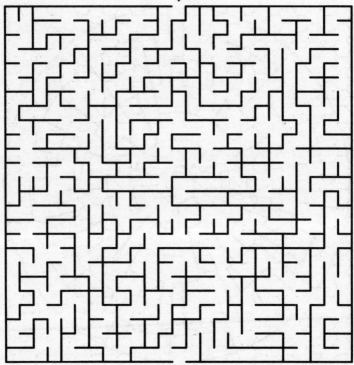

Maze 109

↓ In

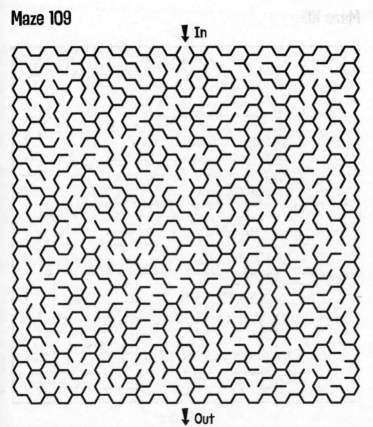

↓ Out

Maze 110

 In

↓ Out

Maze 111

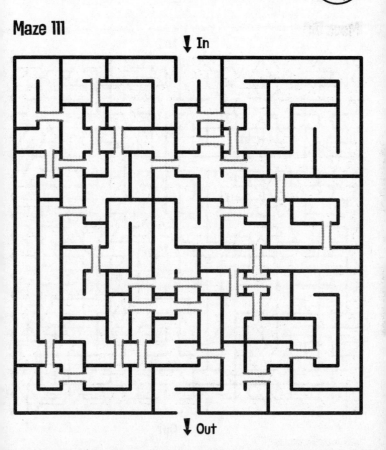

Maze 112

Maze 113

↓ In

↓ Out

Maze 114

Maze 115

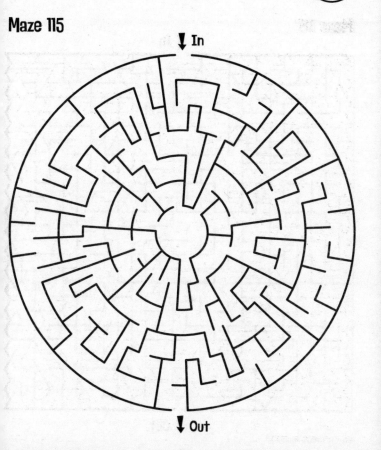

Maze 116

↓ **In**

↓ **Out**

Maze 117

↓ **In**

↓ **Out**

Maze 118

↓ In

↓ Out

Maze 119

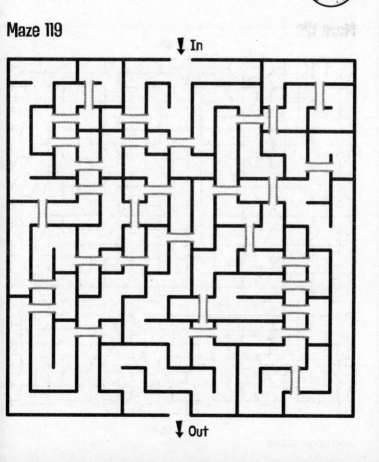

Maze 120

In

Out

Maze 121

In

Out

Maze 122

In

Out

Maze 123

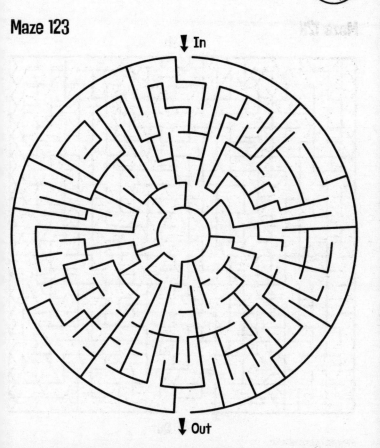

Maze 124

Maze 125

↓ In

↓ Out

Level Four:
Ace Puzzlers

Maze 126

Maze 127

 In

Out

Maze 128

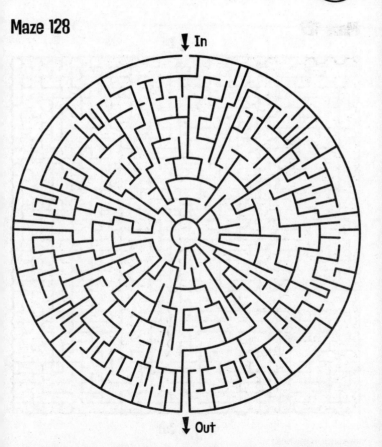

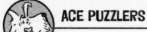

Maze 129

In

Out

Maze 130

↓ **In**

↓ **Out**

Maze 131

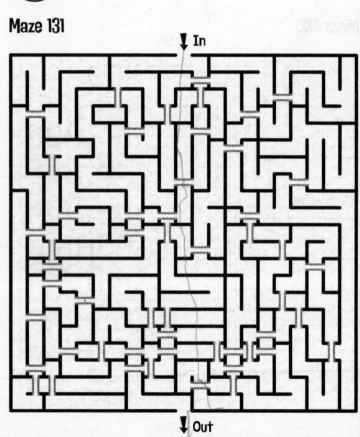

Maze 132

↓ In

↓ Out

Maze 133

↓ **In**

↓ **Out**

Maze 134

↓ In

↓ Out

ACE PUZZLERS Time ....

Maze 135

↓ **In**

↓ **Out**

Maze 136

▼ In

▼ Out

Maze 137

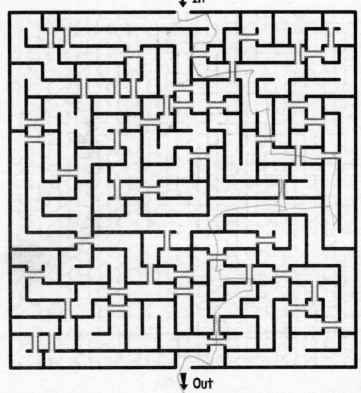

In

Out

Maze 138

↓ In

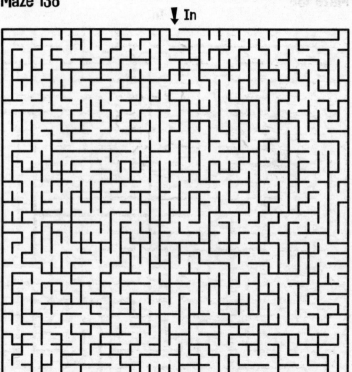

↓ Out

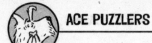

Maze 139

Maze 140

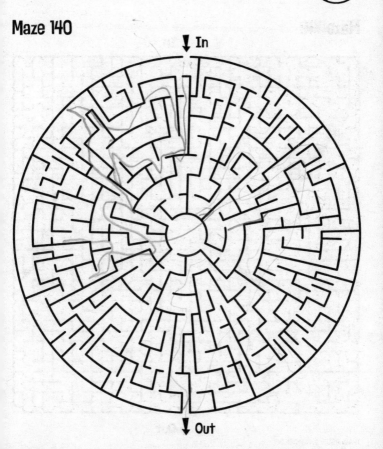

Maze 141

Maze 142

↓ In

↓ Out

Maze 143

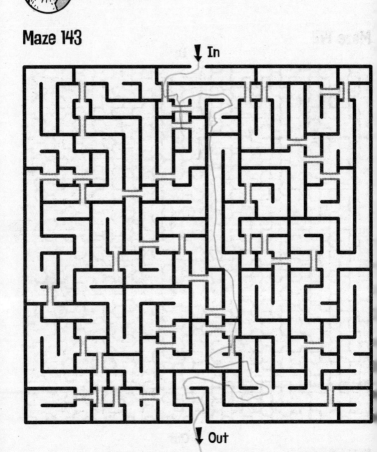

Maze 144

↓ In

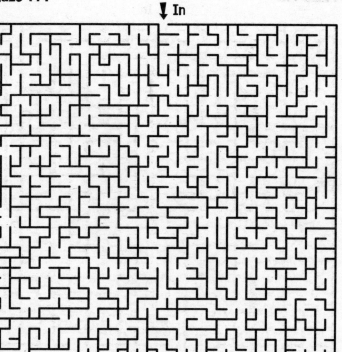

↓ Out

Maze 145

↓ In

↓ Out

Maze 146

↓ In

↓ Out

Maze 147

↓ In

↓ Out

Maze 148

↓ In

↓ Out

Time...........................

Maze 149

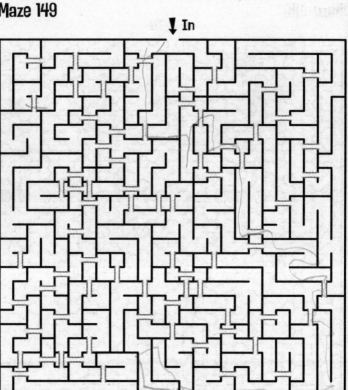

Time ....

Maze 150

↓ In

↓ Out

Maze 151

Maze 152

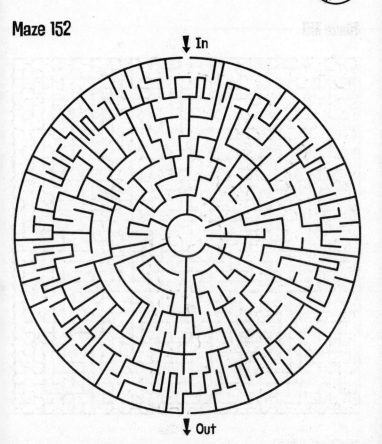

Maze 153

Answers

Beginners

Maze 1

Maze 2

Maze 3

Maze 4

Maze 5

Maze 6

Maze 7

Maze 8

Maze 9

Maze 10

Maze 11
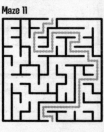

Maze 12

Maze 13

Maze 14

Maze 15

Maze 16

Maze 17

Maze 18

Maze 19

Maze 20

Maze 21

Intermediates

Maze 22

Maze 23

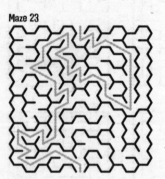

Maze 24

Maze 25

Maze 26

Maze 27

Maze 28

Maze 29

Maze 30

Maze 31

Maze 32

Maze 33

Maze 34

Maze 35

Maze 36

Maze 37

Maze 38

Maze 39

Maze 40

Maze 41

Maze 42

Maze 43

Maze 44

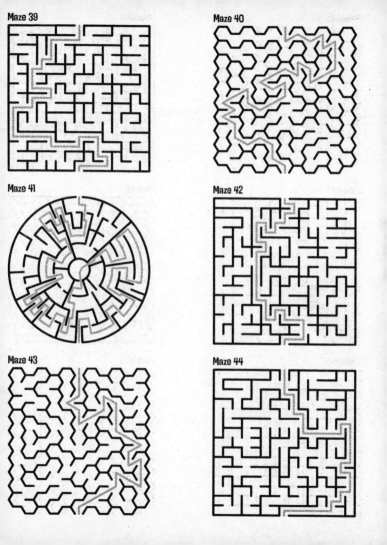

Maze 45

Maze 46

Maze 47

Maze 48

Maze 49

Maze 50

Maze 51

Maze 52

Maze 53

Maze 54

Maze 55

Maze 56

Maze 57

Maze 58

Maze 59

Maze 60

Maze 61

Maze 62

Maze 63

Maze 64

Maze 65

Maze 66

Maze 67

Maze 68

Advanced

Maze 69

Maze 70

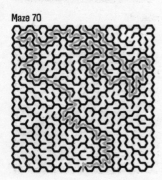

Maze 71

Maze 72

Maze 73

Maze 74

Maze 75

Maze 76

Maze 77

Maze 78

Maze 79

Maze 80

Maze 81

Maze 82

Maze 83

Maze 84

Maze 85

Maze 86

Maze 87

Maze 88

Maze 89

Maze 90

Maze 91

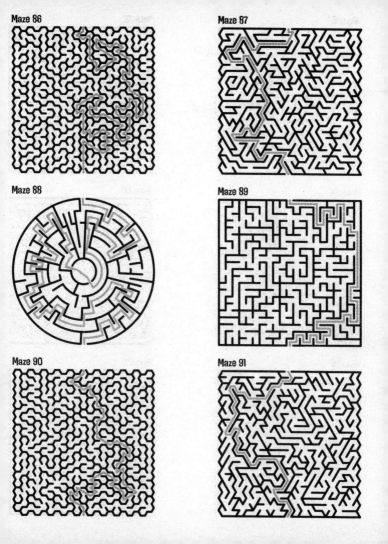

Maze 92

Maze 93

Maze 94

Maze 95

Maze 96

Maze 97

Maze 98

Maze 99

Maze 100

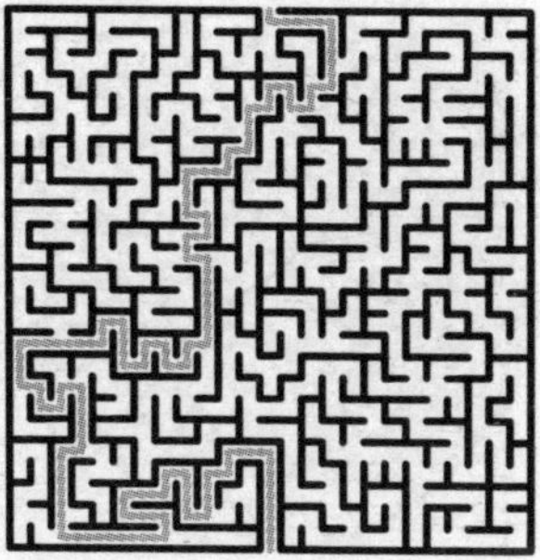

Maze 101

Maze 102

Maze 103

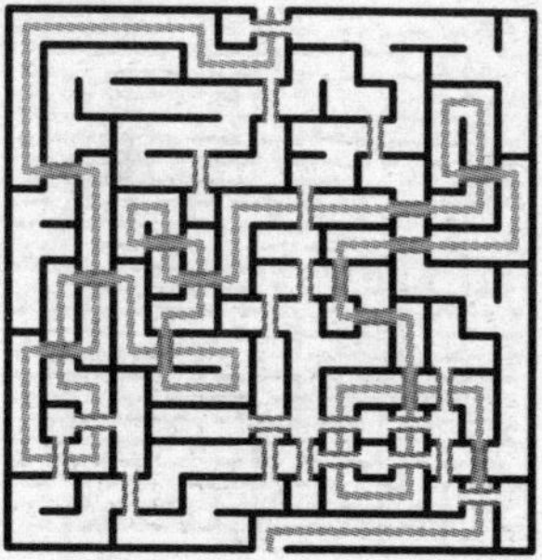

Maze 104

Maze 105

Maze 106

Maze 107

Maze 108

Maze 109

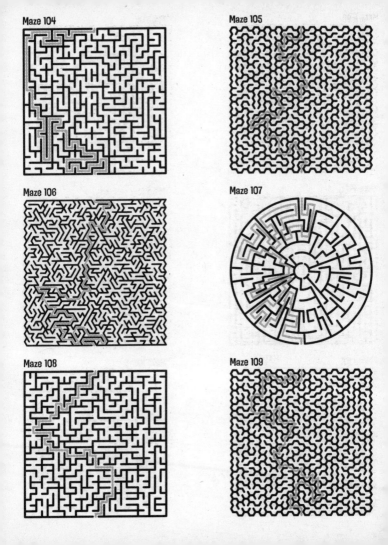

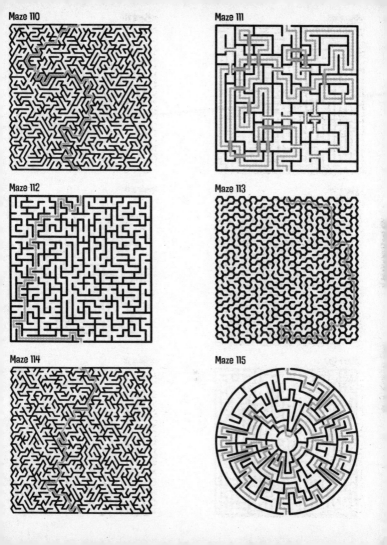

Maze 110

Maze 111

Maze 112

Maze 113

Maze 114

Maze 115

Maze 116

Maze 117

Maze 118

Maze 119

Maze 120

Maze 121

Maze 122

Maze 123

Maze 124

Maze 125

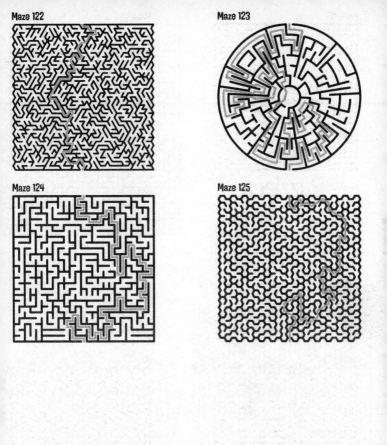

Ace
Puzzlers

Maze 126

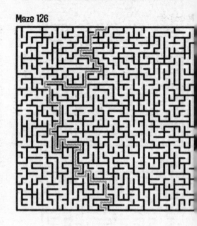

Maze 127

Maze 128

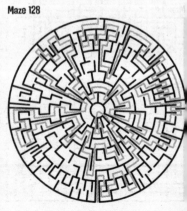

Maze 129

Maze 130

Maze 131

Maze 132

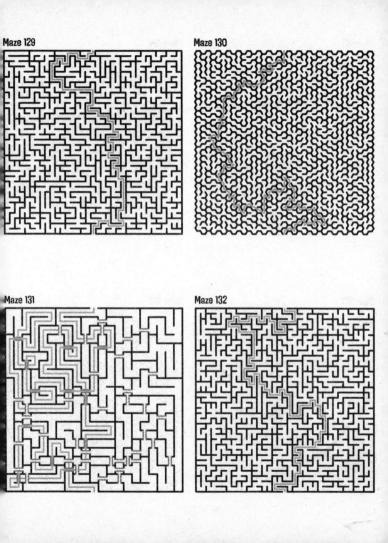

Maze 133

Maze 134

Maze 135

Maze 136

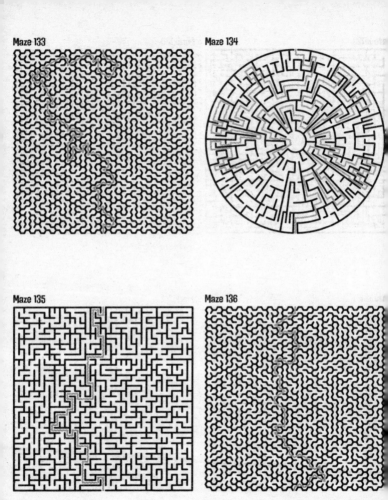

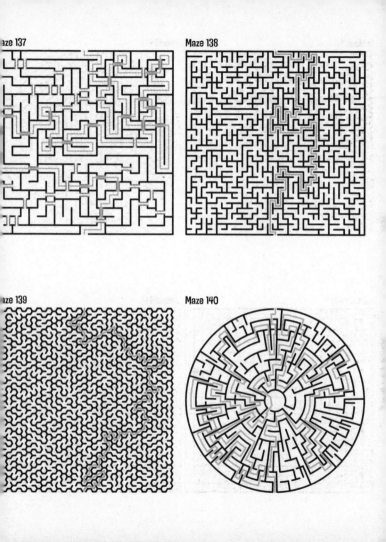

Maze 141

Maze 142

Maze 143

Maze 144

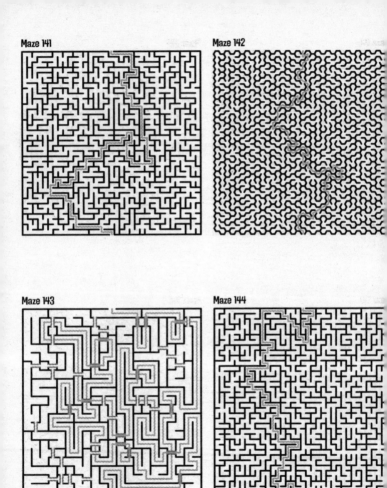

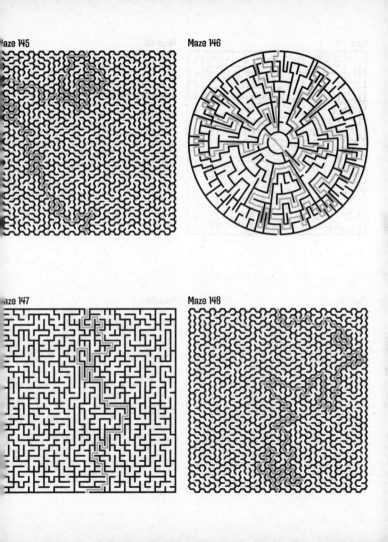

Maze 145

Maze 146

Maze 147

Maze 148

Maze 149

Maze 150

Maze 151

Maze 152

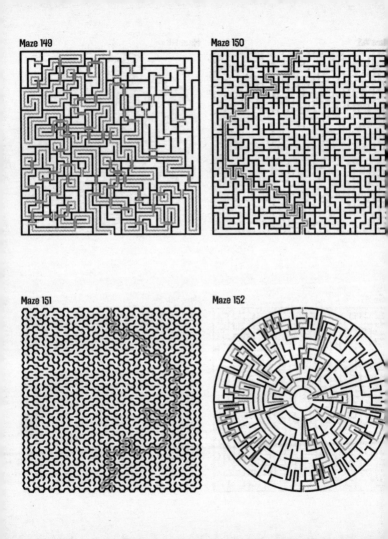

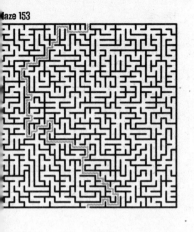